GAITHER

MW00449886

Arranged for Easy Piano by Carol Tornquist

Now you can play the music from church that you love to hear and sing with the *Pure & Simple* series. Each book features lyrics, suggested fingerings, phrasing, pedal markings, and easy-to-read notation. The solo piano arrangements, which use familiar harmonies and rhythms, will put your favorite melodies at your fingertips quickly and easily.

This volume features the gospel music of Bill and Gloria Gaither. These classics have been featured on the popular Gaither Home-coming television specials and on their website, www.gaither.com, making contemporary gospel music available to a wide audience. Their memorable lyrics and melodies have influenced generations of Christian artists and have inspired countless listeners.

Produced by
Alfred Music Publishing Co., Inc.
P.O. Box 10003
Van Nuys, CA 91410-0003
alfred.com

Printed in USA.

ISBN-10: 0-7390-8184-5
ISBN-13: 978-0-7390-8184-6

Cover Photo: © Nancy Bailey-Pratt

CONTENTS

COME, HOLY SPIRIT

Words by William J. and Gloria Gaither
Music by William J. Gaither
Arranged by Carol Tornquist

Slowly, with expression

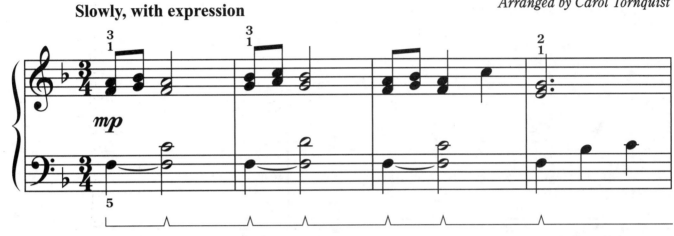

1. Come as a wis-dom to chil-dren.
2., 3. *See additional lyrics*

Verse 2:
Come as a rest to the weary.
Come as a balm for the sore.
Come as a dew to my dryness.
Fill me with joy evermore.

Verse 3:
Come like a spring in the desert.
Come to the withered of soul.
Oh, let Your sweet healing power
Touch me and make me whole.

Because He Lives

Words by William J. and Gloria Gaither
Music by William J. Gaither
Arranged by Carol Tornquist

Moderately slow

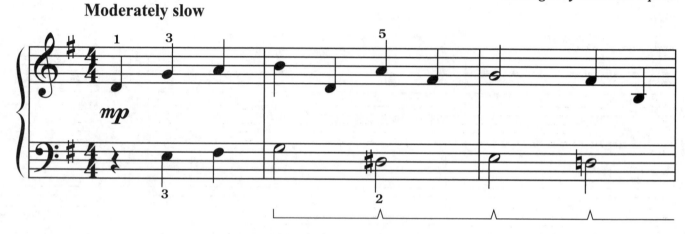

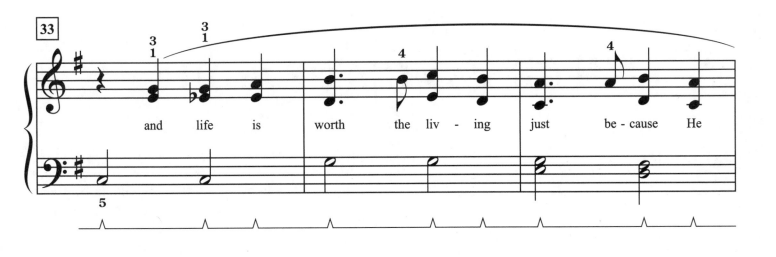

and life is worth the liv - ing just be - cause He

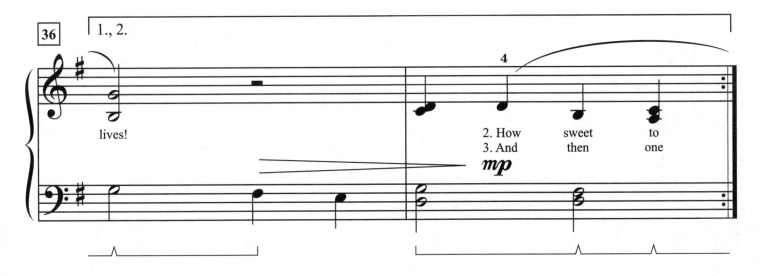

1., 2.

lives!

mp

2. How sweet then to one
3. And then to one

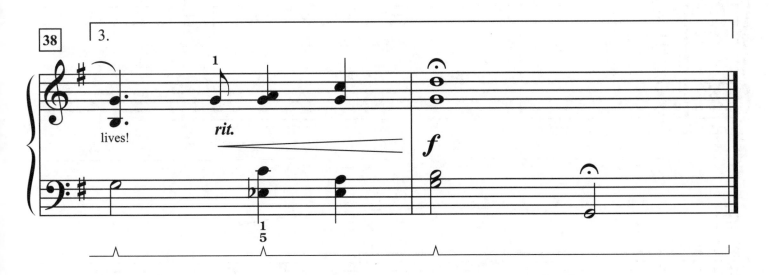

3.

lives!

rit.

f

Verse 3:
And then one day I'll cross that river;
I'll fight life's final war with pain.
And then as death gives way to vict'ry,
I'll see the lights of glory
And I'll know He reigns.

THE FAMILY OF GOD

Words by William J. and Gloria Gaither
Music by William J. Gaither
Arranged by Carol Tornquist

Moderately slow, gently

I'm so glad I'm a part of the fam-'ly of God! I've been washed in the foun-tain, cleansed by His blood.

GENTLE SHEPHERD

Words by Gloria Gaither
Music by William J. Gaither
Arranged by Carol Tornquist

Slowly

Gen - tle Shep - herd,_____ come and

lead us,_____ for we need You to

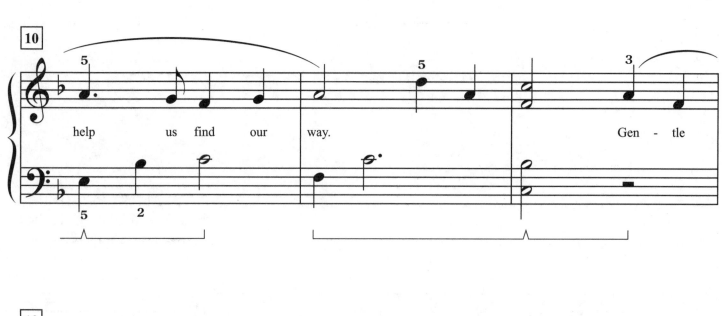

help us find our way. Gen - tle

Shep - herd, ____ come and feed us, ____ for we

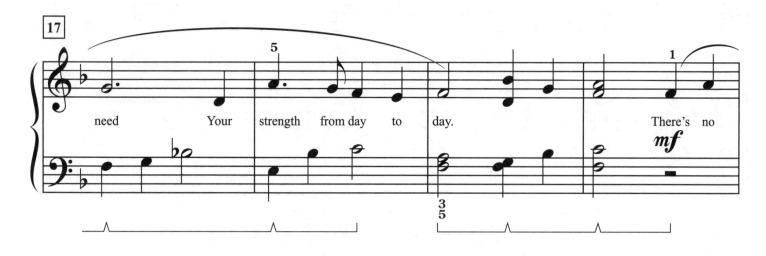

need Your strength from day to day. There's no

mf

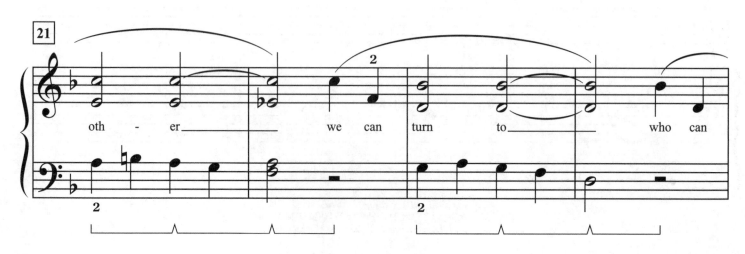

oth - er ____ we can turn to ____ who can

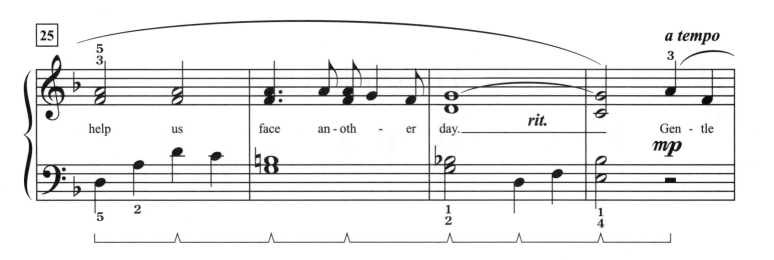

help us face an-oth-er day. *rit.* Gen-tle

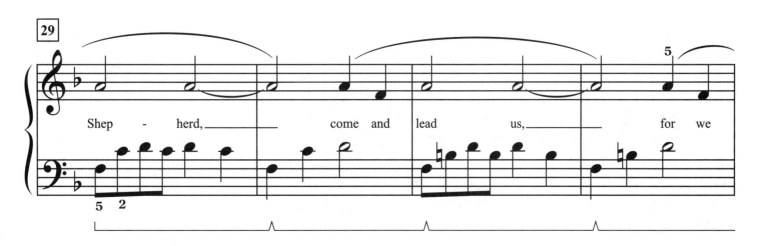

Shep-herd, come and lead us, for we

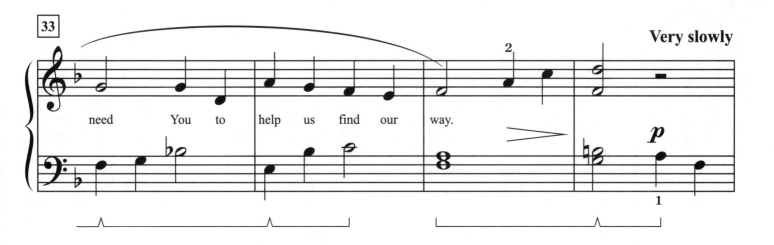

need You to help us find our way.

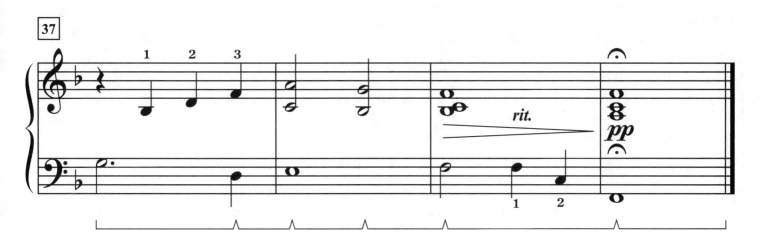

He Started the Whole World Singing

Words by Gloria Gaither
Music by William J. Gaither and Chris Waters
Arranged by Carol Tornquist

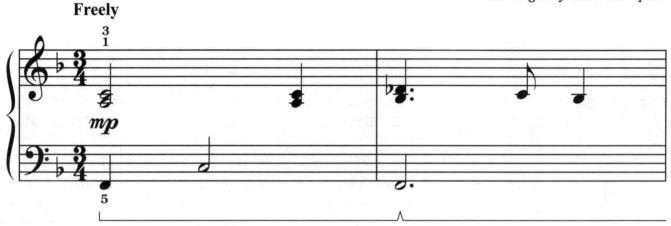

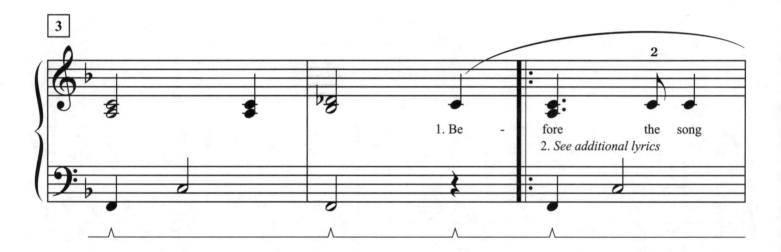

1. Be - fore the song
2. *See additional lyrics*

start - ed, the world, bro - ken - heart - ed, was

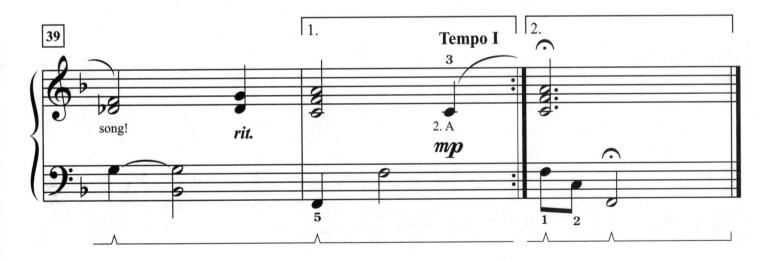

Verse 2:
A new Word was spoken, and chords that were broken
Wove gently together to make a new song.
It was more than a carol to greet the new morn,
For the Source of all music was born!

HE TOUCHED ME

Words and Music by William J. Gaither
Arranged by Carol Tornquist

Moderately, with reverence

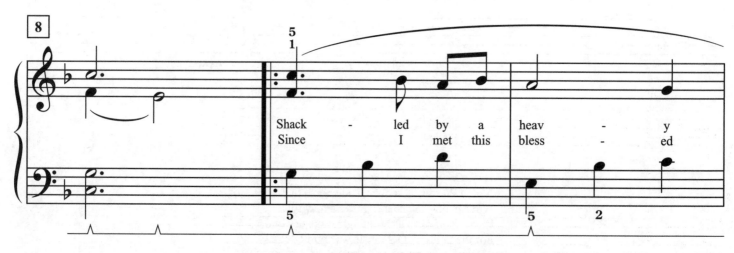

22

I Am Loved

Words by William J. and Gloria Gaither
Music by William J. Gaither
Arranged by Carol Tornquist

21

mp

1. All I had to bring was im - per - fec - tion.

2., 3. *See additional lyrics*

24

There was so much more I lacked than I pos -

27

sessed.   I could hard - ly

30

com - pre - hend His of - fer:

Verse 2:
I said, "If You knew, You wouldn't want me;
My scars are hidden by the face I wear."
He said, "My child, My scars go deeper;
It was love for you that put them there."

Verse 3:
Forgiven, I repeat it, I'm forgiven;
Clean before my Lord I freely stand.
Forgiven, I can dare forgive my brother;
Forgiven, I reach out to take your hand.

Last Chorus:
You are loved, you are loved,
You can risk loving, too,
For the One who knows you best loves you most.
You are loved, you are loved.
Won't you please take our hand?
We are free to love each other,
We are loved!

I Believe in a Hill Called Mount Calvary

Words by William J. and Gloria Gaither and Dale Oldham
Music by William J. Gaither
Arranged by Carol Tornquist

I WILL SERVE THEE

Words by William J. and Gloria Gaither
Music by William J. Gaither
Arranged by Carol Tornquist

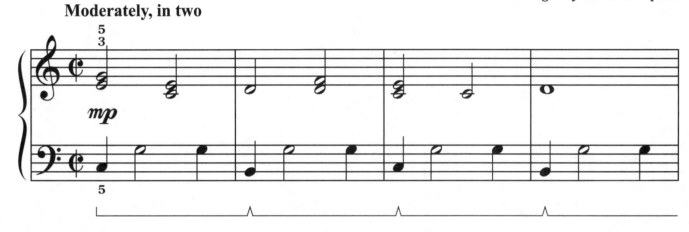

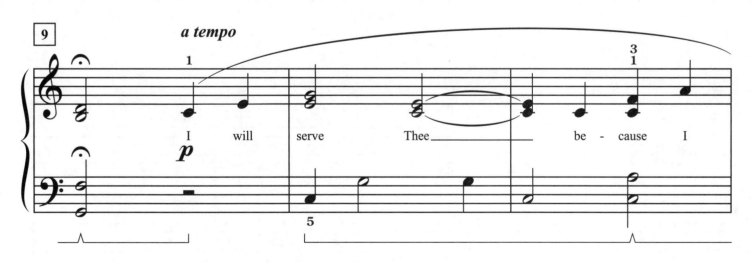

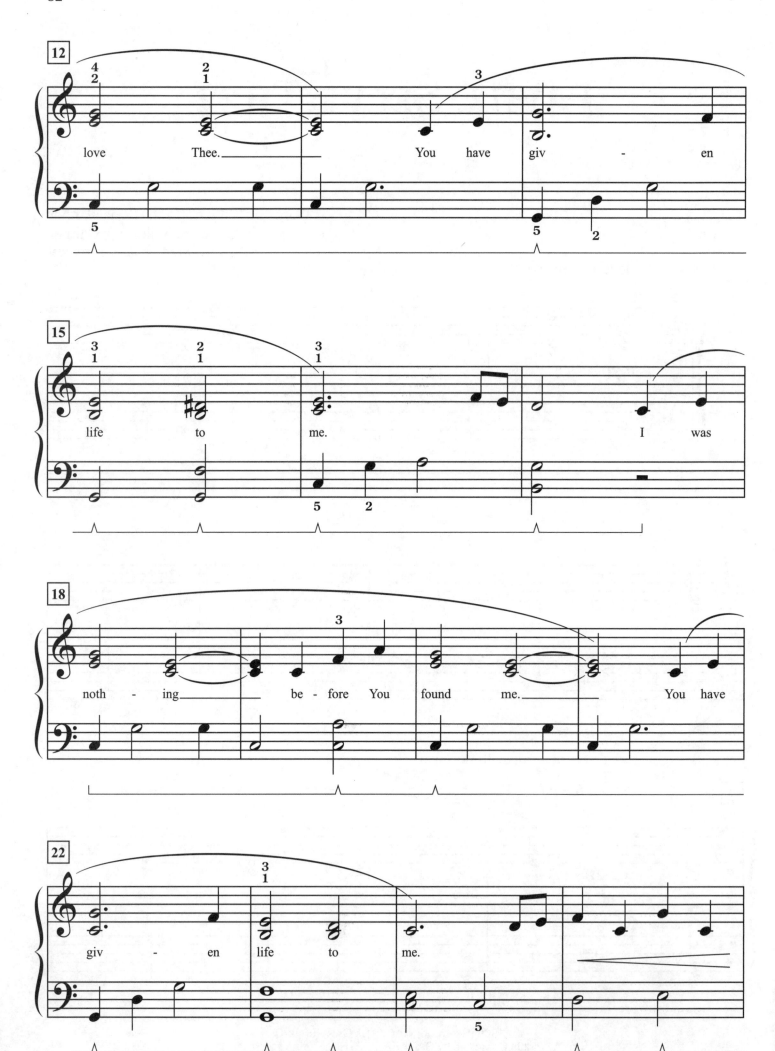

It Is Finished

Words by William J. and Gloria Gaither
Music by William J. Gaither
Arranged by Carol Tornquist

IT WILL BE WORTH IT ALL

Words and Music by William J. Gaither
Arranged by Carol Tornquist

I've Just Seen Jesus

Words by Gloria Gaither
Music by William J. Gaither and Danny Daniels
Arranged by Carol Tornquist

Jesus, We Just Want to Thank You

Words by William J. and Gloria Gaither
Music by William J. Gaither
Arranged by Carol Tornquist

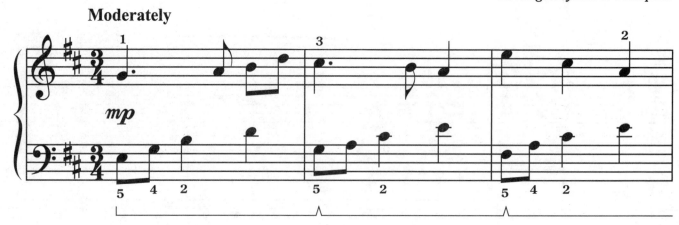

1. Je - sus, we
3. *See additional lyrics*

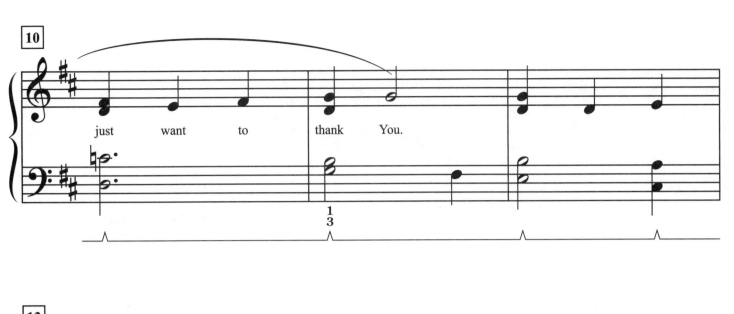

just want to thank You.

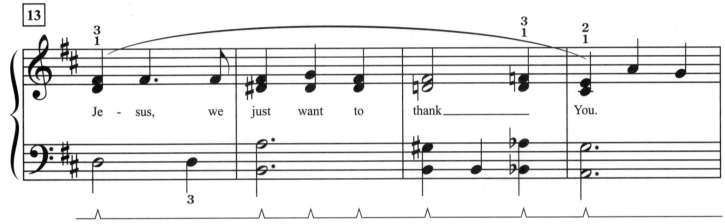

Je - sus, we just want to thank_____ You.

Je - sus, we just want to thank You.

Thank You for be - ing so good.

46

Verse 3:
Jesus, we just want to tell You,
Jesus, we just want to tell You,
Jesus, we just want to tell You,
We love You for being so good.

Verse 4:
Savior, we just want to serve You,
Savior, we just want to serve You,
Savior, we just want to serve You,
Serve You for being so good.

Verse 5:
Jesus, we know You are coming,
Jesus, we know You are coming,
Jesus, we know You are coming,
Take us to live in Your home.

Jesus Is Lord of All

Words by William J. and Gloria Gaither
Music by William J. Gaither
Arranged by Carol Tornquist

Slowly, with expression

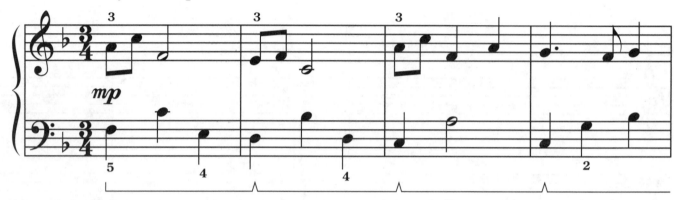

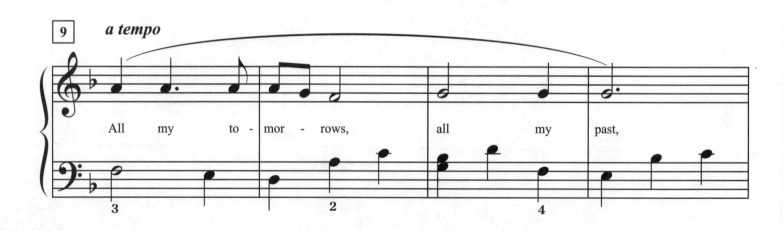

Je - sus is Lord_____ of all.

I've quit my strug - gles, con - tent - ment at last,

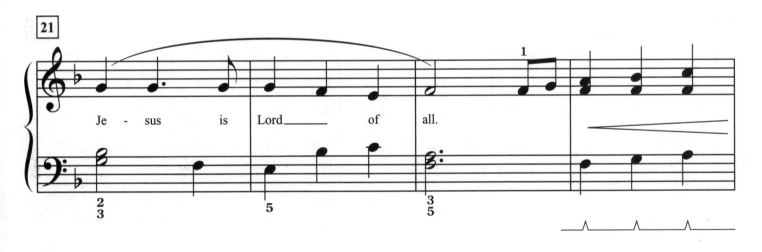

Je - sus is Lord_____ of all.

King of kings, Lord of lords,

THE KING IS COMING

Words by William J. and Gloria Gaither and Charles Millhuff
Music by William J. Gaither
Arranged by Carol Tornquist

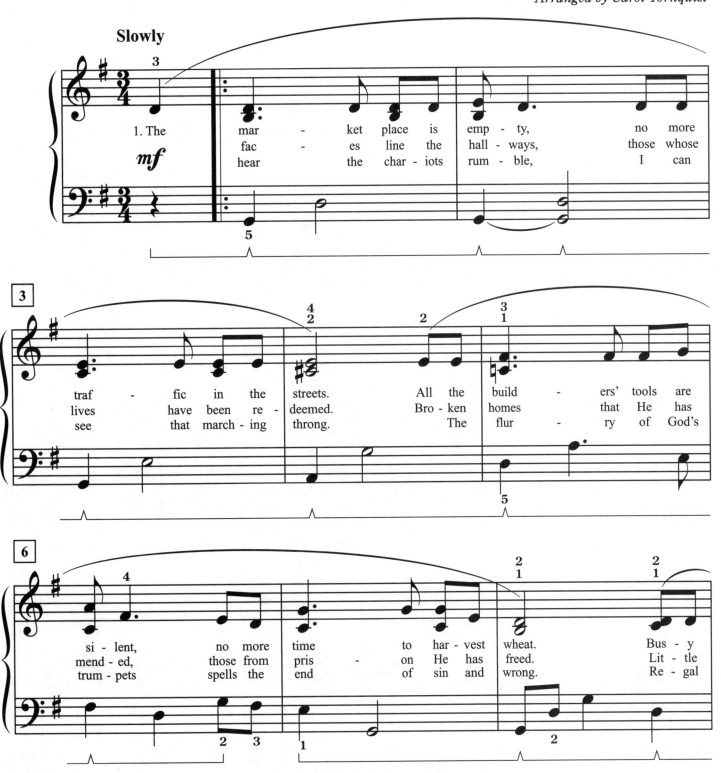

LET'S JUST PRAISE THE LORD

Words by William J. and Gloria Gaither
Music by William J. Gaither
Arranged by Carol Tornquist

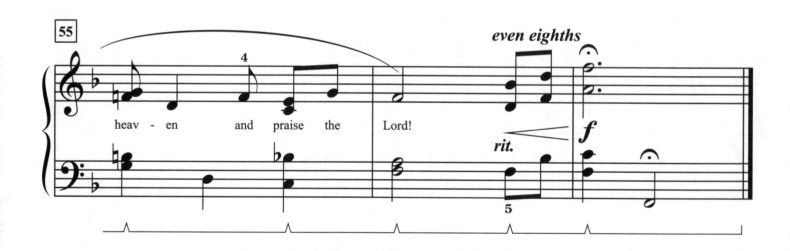

Verse 2:
Just the precious name of Jesus is worthy of our praise;
Let us bow our knees before Him, our hands to heaven raise.
When He comes in clouds of glory, with Him we'll ever reign,
So let's lift our happy voices and praise His name.

The Longer I Serve Him

Words and Music by William J. Gaither
Arranged by Carol Tornquist

13
since I gave my heart to Je - sus, the
Ev - 'ry day my way gets bright - er, the
17
long - er I serve___ Him, the sweet - er He
long - er I serve___ Him, the sweet - er He
20
grows.
grows.
The
mf
long - er I serve Him, the
23
sweet - er He grows. The more that I

SOMETHING BEAUTIFUL

Words by Gloria Gaither
Music by William J. Gaither
Arranged by Carol Tornquist

Slowly, with expression

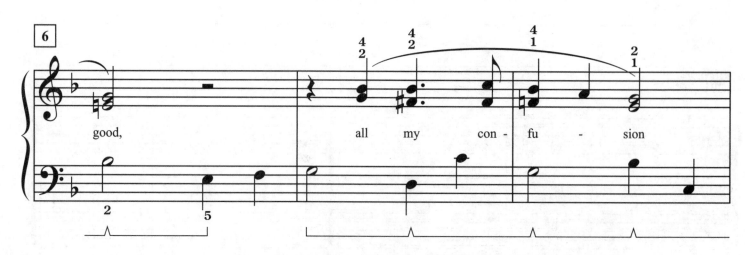

21 they were my dreams at the start; and the hopes for life's best were the

24 hopes that I har-bored down deep in my heart. But my

27 dreams turned to ash-es, my cas-tles all crum-bled, my

29 for-tune turned to loss. So I wrapped it all in the

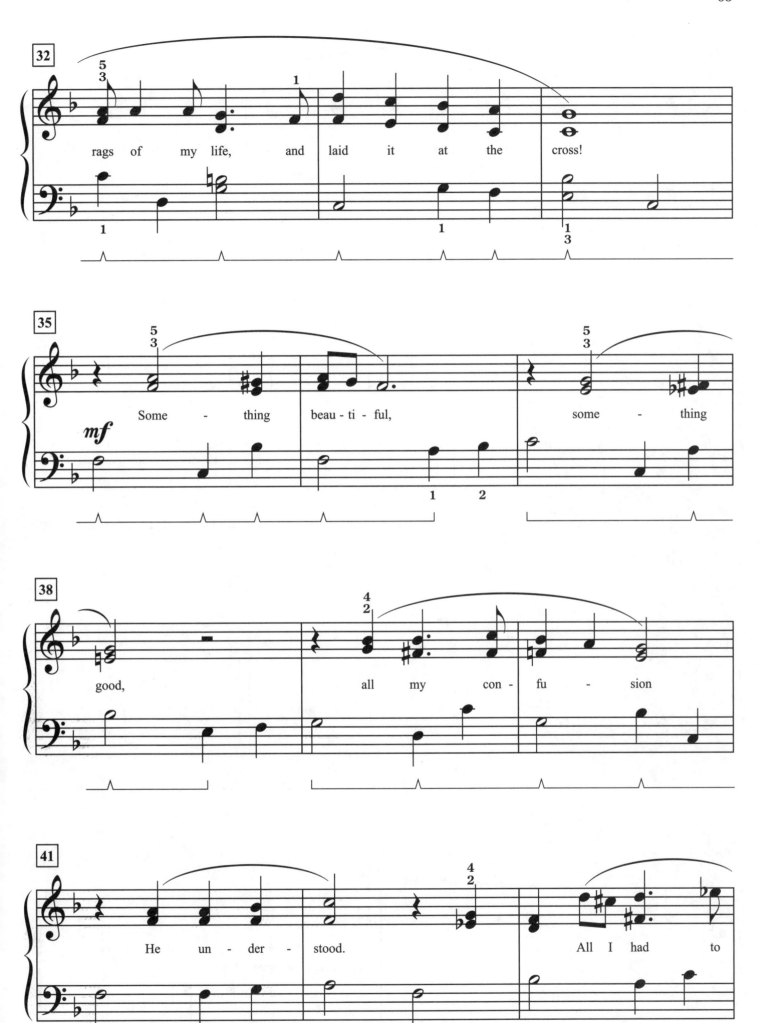

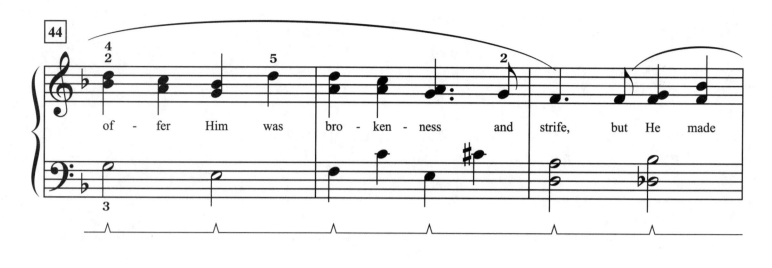

of - fer Him was bro - ken - ness and strife, but He made

some - thing beau - ti - ful of my life.

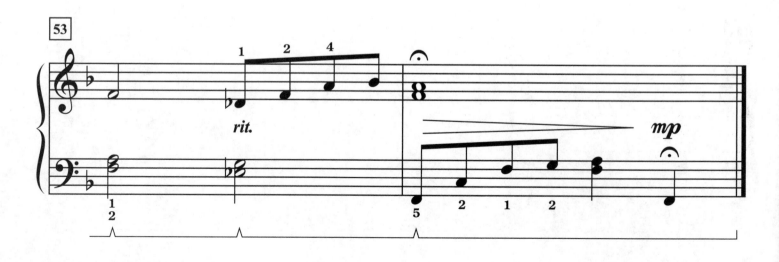

There's Something About That Name

Words by William J. and Gloria Gaither
Music by William J. Gaither
Arranged by Carol Tornquist

Moderately slow, with reverence

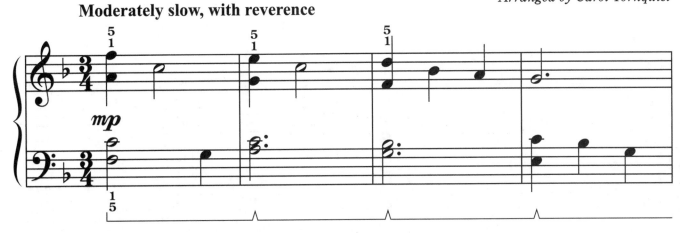

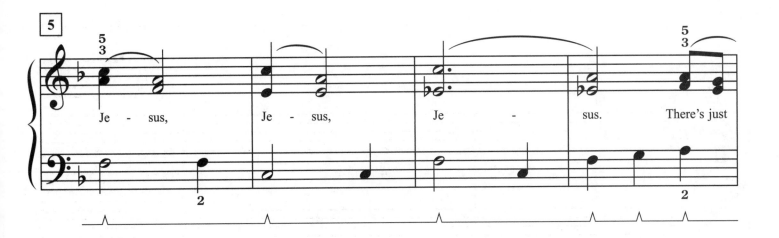

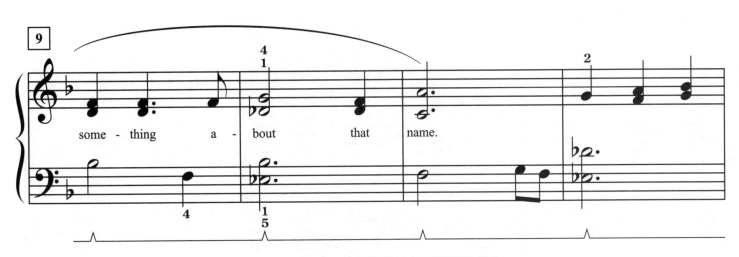

earth pro - claim:

kings and king - doms will all pass a -

way, but there's some - thing a - bout that

name. *cresc.* *mf*

THEN CAME THE MORNING

Words by Gloria Gaither
Music by William J. Gaither and Chris Christian
Arranged by Carol Tornquist

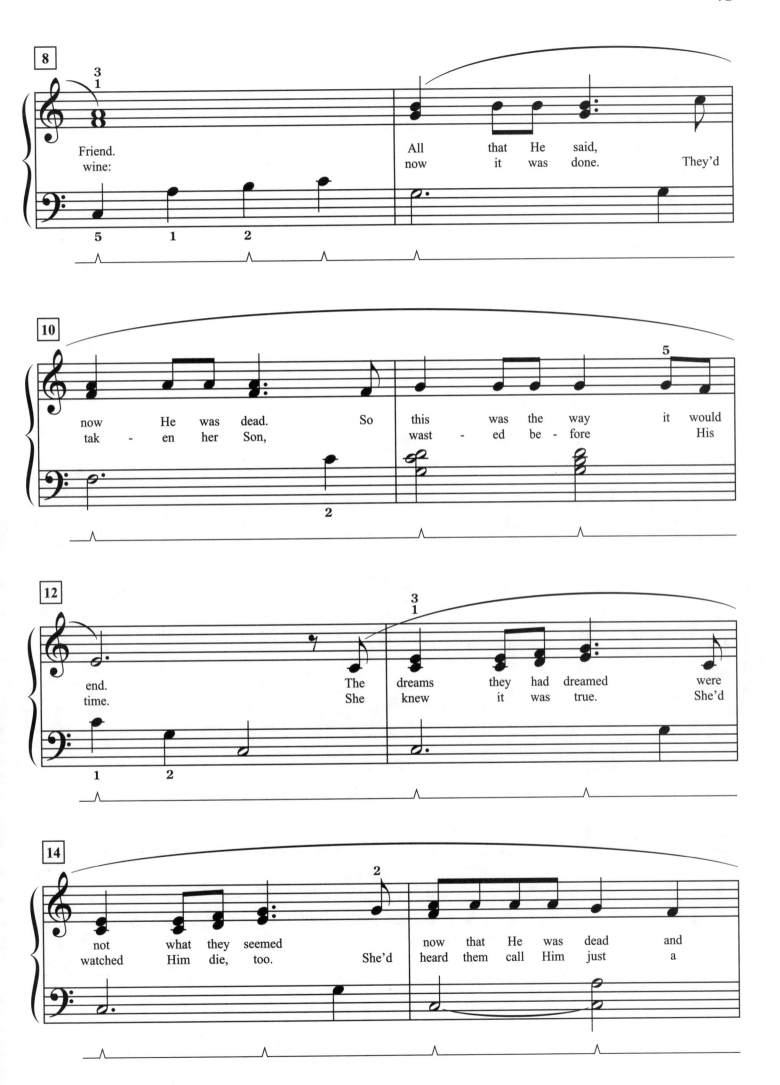

THESE ARE THEY

Words by William J. and Gloria Gaither
Music by William J. Gaither
Arranged by Carol Tornquist

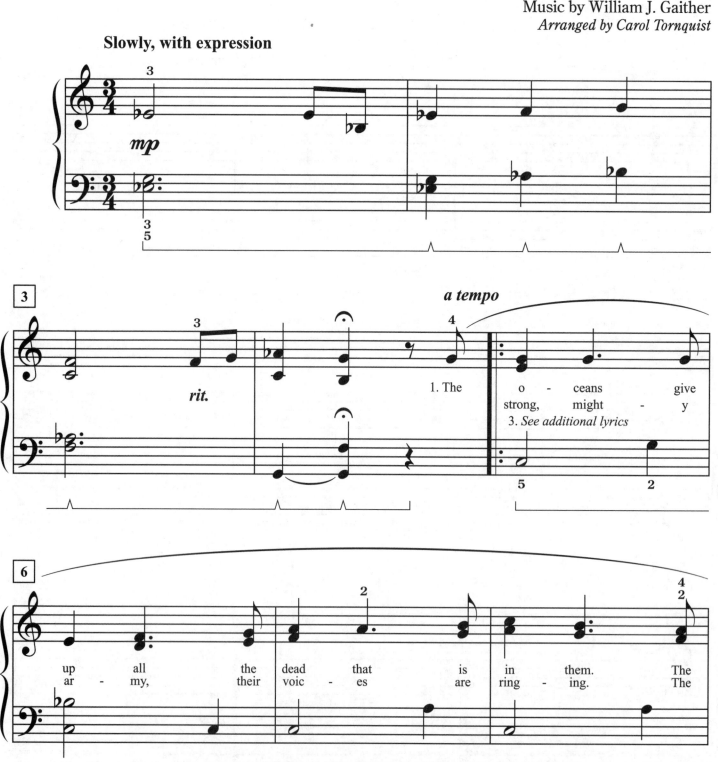

Verse 3:
All the strangers and pilgrims are no longer strangers,
And the tired, weary wanderers wander no more.
The table is spread for the great celebration,
And the "Welcome Home" banner flies over the door.

WE HAVE THIS MOMENT, TODAY

Words by Gloria Gaither
Music by William J. Gaither
Arranged by Carol Tornquist

Moderately slow, gently

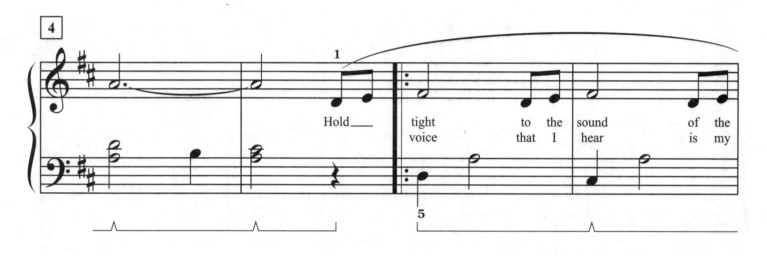

Hold tight to the voice that I hear sound of the is my

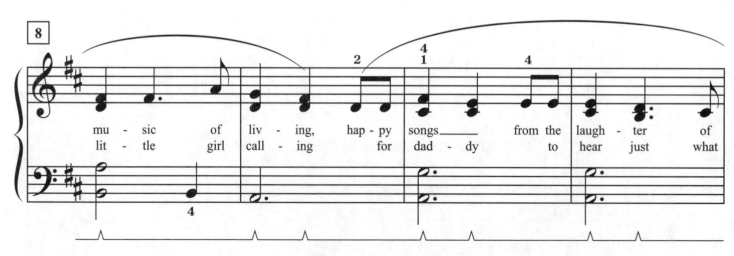

mu - sic of liv - ing, hap - py songs from the laugh - ter of
lit - tle girl call - ing for dad - dy to hear just what